People Who Met Jesus

7 Seeker Bible Discussions

Rebecca Manley Pippert

InterVarsity Press
Downers Grove, Illinois
Leicester, England

InterVarsity Press, USA
P.O. Box 1400, Downers Grove, IL 60515-1426, USA
World Wide Web: www.ivpress.com
E-mail: mail@ivpress.com

Inter-Varsity Press, England
38 De Montfort Street, Leicester LE1 7GP, England
World Wide Web: www.ivpbooks.com
E-mail: ivp@uccf.org.uk

InterVarsity Press®, U.S.A., is the book-publishing division of InterVarsity Christian Fellowship/USA®, a student movement active on campus at hundreds of universities, colleges and schools of nursing in the United States of America, and a member movement of the International Fellowship of Evangelical Students. For information about local and regional activities, write Public Relations Dept., InterVarsity Christian Fellowship/USA, 6400 Schroeder Rd., P.O. Box 7895, Madison, WI 53707-7895, or visit the IVCF website at <www.intervarsity.org>.

Inter-Varsity Press, England, is the book-publishing division of the Universities and Colleges Christian Fellowship (formerly the Inter-Varsity Fellowship), a student movement linking Christian Unions in universities and colleges throughout the United Kingdom and the Republic of Ireland, and a member movement of the International Fellowship of Evangelical Students. For information about local and national activities write to UCCF, 38 De Montfort Street, Leicester LE1 7GP.

Design: Cindy Kiple

Images: Eugene Burnand/Bridgeman Art Library

USA ISBN 0-8308-2126-0

UK ISBN 1-84474-057-9

Printed in the United States of America ∞

P	16	15	14	13	12	11	10	9	8	7	6	5	4	3	2	1
Y	16	15	14	13	12	11	10	09	08	07	06	05	04			

Contents

INTRODUCTION

G. K. Chesterton was once asked to contribute to a series in the *London Times* on the question, "What is the Problem in the universe?" to which he answered, "'I am.' Sincerely, G. K. Chesterton."

The truth is, it doesn't take much observation to recognize the paradox of the human condition: we contain both good and bad, we are both generous and self-centered, both honest and devious. We can look around and see how much genuine kindness there is. We have a capacity for love, an appreciation of beauty, and moments of genuine courage. But unfortunately that's not the whole story. Sooner or later, whether through a difficult relationship, a demanding spouse, a wayward child, or simply through overwhelming or infuriating circumstances, we are confronted with our darker side.

Has it ever struck you as odd that, for all our sophistication, we have a remarkably naive understanding of human nature? We have lived through history's most murderous century, yet we flatter ourselves that we are basically wonderful people who occasionally do bad deeds. The founders of the United States were not so naive. They understood that we were created in God's image, but they were also ruggedly realistic that human nature had a root of evil which left unchecked could grow to terrifying proportions.

The question then, in light of our human dilemma is: Does God make a difference? Can God help those who are frustrated and left with longings because of the gaps in their lives? With God's help and restorative power can we finally overcome our sins and weaknesses or must we always undergo? Is it possible to change? The Bible has the nerve to proclaim: "Yes! And again, Yes!" Those wistful longings of the heart can be met. Those destructive sinful patterns can be conquered by being in relationship with God as King.

Using This Discussion Guide

Since my own journey began in skepticism, where I was encouraged to ask questions and never asked to adopt belief blindly, I have chosen a similar approach in these Bible discussions. It is not necessary that you believe in Jesus or accept the Bible as "divinely inspired" in order to use this guide. Rather, come to the accounts of Jesus as you would to any sound history, with an open mind and heart to see what you find.

This guide is written to encourage give-and-take group discussion led by a moderator. The open-style discussion challenges you as participants to wrestle with the text yourselves and to reach your own conclusions. Don't feel intimidated if this is your first time reading the Bible; that means your contributions to group discussions will be fresh and stimulating. Remember, there is no homework. If you want to answer the questions ahead of time go right ahead (space is provided for writing answers to each question). If you are able to read the passage ahead of time, then do so. But it's also fine to simply show up each week without having prepared ahead of time.

Each session has several components. The "Discussion Starter" question is simply meant to kick off the discussion for a few minutes. The "Historical Context" section is intended to be read aloud. Its purpose is to provide background to the Scripture. Other historical information is found here and there amidst the discussion questions. The "Discovering Jesus" section contains questions that help us engage the text in order to understand its meaning. The "Live What You Learn" section is to help us apply the truth we've studied to our everyday lives.

We are about to read of several people who encountered Jesus and whose lives were changed forever. Most of the studies are taken from the Gospel book of Luke. What fascinated Luke was the realization that there was no person that Jesus could not reach, no boundary that the gospel could not cross. The gospel is for all who will repent, submit and surrender in faith. That is why Luke chose stories that depicted many classes of people who encountered Jesus—not only Jews and Gentiles,

Romans and Samaritans, but widows, cripples and prostitutes as well as the powerful and rich. Luke writes more about women than any other Gospel writer. Luke saw that the good news was for real people with real needs, whether they be slave or free, the elite or those whom society despises—the poor, the weak, the outcast.

Luke was a Gentile, and the only non-Jewish writer of the New Testament. He was concerned about our humanity and his Gospel clearly relates to human need. Luke was also a careful historian who was thorough and painstakingly careful in what he reported. Luke was also a physician by trade. His business was to heal. Luke had a *professional* interest in how Jesus, the Divine Savior and Healer, had come into the world to deliver us from both sickness and sin. What impressed Luke, the author of this Gospel, was how everyone who responded in faith to Jesus found life-changing help.

The stories we are about to read reveal God's tremendous scope of salvation. Indeed Luke was a theologian of salvation. Luke wanted us to see that the true God cares for the whole person—emotionally, spiritually and physically.

ONE

Finding Wholeness

◆ Discussion Starter

How can positive life events create a barrier to faith by keeping us from seeking God?

How can negative life events cause us to doubt God?

◆ Historical Context

In an earlier chapter Jesus identified himself as the one "anointed to preach good news to the poor" (4:18). In this week's and next week's study we will examine Luke 7 in which we see people with diverse backgrounds and varying approaches to Jesus—all different in how they expressed faith in Jesus. What impressed Luke, the author of this Gospel, was not only that Jesus' message was intended for all people but that those who responded to him in even partial faith received the help they were looking for. Jesus' authority was revealed in chapter 6 of Luke; now in chapter 7 we encounter an unlikely seeker with a phenomenal grasp of Jesus' authority.

◆ Discovering Jesus

Jesus and a Roman Official: Read Luke 7:1-10.

1. This centurion was a Gentile Roman army officer in command of 100 soldiers. What do we learn about this man (his nationality, his economic status, the importance of his position, his personal qualities)?

2. Why did the Jewish elders think Jesus should do as the centurion asked (vv. 4-5)?

3. The centurion's action in verses 6-7 revealed that he was culturally sensitive, because Jews believed they would risk ceremonial contamination to enter the home of a Gentile. This centurion had all the authority of imperial Rome behind him, yet why was his view of the situation so different from the Jewish elders (vv. 6-7)?

4. Only twice do the Gospels record that Jesus was

stirred by amazement (v. 9 and Mark 6:6). What evidence of the centurion's extraordinary faith and cultural sensitivity do you see?

5. What difference must the centurion's faith in Jesus have made on the lives of all the people involved?

6. What do we learn about Jesus' scale of values from the fact that he was willing to go to so much trouble, even risking ceremonial contamination, for a Gentile slave?

The Widow of Nain: Read Luke 7:11-17.

7. Picture the two crowds in verses 11-13 meeting just outside the town gate. If you were in the crowd with Jesus, try to imagine what you would have seen and heard. What would have been the difference in mood between the two groups?

8. How would the woman's future have been affected by this bereavement (v. 12)?

9. There is no request for help, no mention of the widow's faith. What do you think motivated Jesus to respond as powerfully he did (v. 13)?

10. To touch the coffin of a dead person would make a person ceremonially unclean in the eyes of the Jews. What would have been the reaction of the crowds on seeing Jesus, a rabbi, actually touch the coffin?

11. How did Jesus restore the young man to life (v. 14)?

12. What was the response of the crowd (vv. 16-17)?

13. Luke placed the story of the Roman centurion, who had wealth and massive resources at his fingertips, next to the story of the widow who had no resources and no future. What do these stories about two very different people reveal about human inadequacy and Jesus' power to overcome?

◆ Live What You Learn

Salvation is a rich word in the Bible that has several meanings. It means "reconciled to God," but it also means making whole what has been broken, rescuing what is lost and forgiving what is sinful. As a physician Luke was constantly amazed by the power of Jesus' healing ministry. He saw that contact with Jesus, when there was some response of faith, made people whole in the ways they most needed to be whole—be it spiritual, emotional or physical. What impressed Luke above all else was that Jesus was the "Savior of the world" who came to redeem and rescue people who were in trouble and needed help. In the case of the centurion his faith in Jesus enabled his slave to be healed. In the case of the widow her grief was so great that it didn't occur to her to ask for such a miracle. Today, as well, believers testify to Christ's healing power—be it through physical healing or experiencing his peace and joy even in the midst of difficult trials. Christ's touch brings spiritual wholeness.

Aristotle Onassis, the late Greek shipping magnate who was once considered the richest man in the world, developed a rare incurable disease that forced him to use bandages to keep his eyelids from drooping. He also battled depression when his adult son died in a plane crash. "I am the richest man in the world, yet I couldn't save my son from dying any more than I could save myself from this disease. It feels so hopeless."

14. Coming to the realization that we can't control the things that matter most caused Onassis to despair. What do you think the centurion would say to Onassis about why there is reason for hope?

15. What have you thought you could control that you learned you could not?

TWO

Faith's Authentic Response

◆ Discussion Starter

If someone said to you, "I couldn't go to God, not after all I have done," how would you answer that person?

◆ Historical Context

Last week we saw that for all his power, wealth and prestige, the centurion could not help his dying servant—only Jesus could. The widow was equally powerless in the face of her son's death. Jesus' extravagant response in meeting their needs wasn't based on what they had done to earn it but on his unconditional love and mercy. Salvation, then, is not achieved through our personal merit but by God's grace through our faith in Christ. Today we continue in chapter seven with two people who show us the other side of the story: while salvation is not based on personal merit, once it is received it *must* lead to good works.

The Pharisees were one of the two major political religious factions. They were conservative and traditionally religious. They were becoming increasingly critical of Jesus, and some were envious of his healing power and popularity. They were especially angered when Jesus pronounced forgiveness of sin to a paralytic (Luke 5:17-20). Many had come to Capernaum to interrogate Jesus because of his claim to be Messiah, the long-awaited King that God had promised.

The setting of this story is in the house of a wealthy Pharisee. Their houses were built in the Roman style with a large room where tables and couches were set up. Sometimes they set up the furniture in the courtyard, particularly when there were special guests. Uninvited people could come and stand around the sides of the courtyard and watch and listen, but they were not invited to eat. This seems to be the situation of this story where Jesus is the special guest of honor.

◆ Discovering Jesus

Jesus at Simon's Banquet: Read Luke 7:36-50.

1. Why do you think Simon invited Jesus to this banquet?

2. Simon failed to show three obligatory Middle Eastern courtesies (vv. 44-46). This was obviously not an oversight. What do you think was Simon's intention?

3. Take the point of view of Simon (see v. 39) and describe what you see happening in verses 37-38.

   What do you think Simon, a righteous Jew, would have felt?

4. What information do we have about the woman who is the main character in this story?

5. Considering the enormous trust issues this woman must have had with men, why do you think she began to weep when she arrived near Jesus?

6. Jesus knew that to be touched by any woman in public, let alone a prostitute, would damage his reputation. Why didn't Jesus stop her and ask that she express her gratitude in a more "socially correct" way?

7. Why was Simon certain that Jesus couldn't have been a real prophet?

8. In Jesus' story, one debtor owed the equivalent of two years' salary, and the other debtor owed the equivalent of two months' salary. What was Jesus trying to get Simon to realize by telling him this story?

9. What did the woman's extravagant actions upon entering the party reveal about what had happened

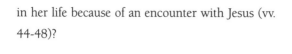

in her life because of an encounter with Jesus (vv. 44-48)?

10. Jesus was showing Simon that love does not earn forgiveness but results from it (vv. 44-48). Therefore, if faith (v. 50), gratitude and affection to Christ are the evidence of one's spiritual state, then what did Simon's ingratitude reveal about him?

11. How do the other guests react when Jesus declares the woman's sins are forgiven (v. 49)?

12. What effect would it have had on this woman and her place in the community that Jesus publicly commended her faith (v. 50)?

13. What can we learn from this passage about how we demonstrate evidence for our salvation?

Women Join Jesus' Team: Read Luke 8:1-3.

As Jesus continued on his preaching tours through villages and towns there were several women who followed him. Socially, these women were a mixed group. One of them came from the privileged class; others Jesus had saved from evil spirits and diseases. Mary from Magdala had been delivered of seven evil spirits. Later she was the first one Jesus appeared to after his resurrection.

14. How did the women who accompanied Jesus and his team express their faith and devotion?

15. When faith is genuinely experienced what is the inevitable fruit that results?

▶ Live What You Learn

16. Consider the four individuals we have encountered in the past two weeks: The centurion was a powerful commander who had amazing faith. The grief-stricken widow had passive or implicit faith. Simon, the wealthy Pharisee of social position, was a skeptical seeker, and the social outcast—probably a reformed prostitute—had a lavish and grateful love for Christ because she knew she was forgiven. Which of these characters do you most readily identify with and why?

THREE

The Essence of True Religion

◆ Discussion Starter

Augustine, the famous Christian thinker from the third century, wrote: "My sin was all the more incurable because I did not think myself a sinner." Do you think we live in an age that could resonate with this statement? Why or why not?

◆ Historical Context

In the preceding passage, Jesus said that understanding was given to the spiritually responsive, by grace. Intellectual ability is neither an advantage nor a disadvantage, but pride is the obstacle. The lawyer we are about to meet is a case in point when Jesus told one of his most famous stories: the parable of the "Good Samaritan."

The word *parable* is a comparison or illustration, commonly given as a story in the New Testament. Jesus used them to convey a core spiritual truth. There are forty parables recorded in Matthew, Mark and Luke (the Gospel of John does not contain any parables).

One of the most important things to pay attention to when reading a parable is who the parable is directed toward. Knowing Jesus' audience will enable us to grasp the parable's deeper meaning. In this case the parable of the good Samaritan is given to a sophisticated, proud lawyer who was an expert in Old Testament law and its application.

Discovering Jesus

Jesus and the Lawyer: Read Luke 10:25-37.

1. What was the motive given behind the lawyer's question (v. 25)?

2. His first question to Jesus was: "What must I *do* to inherit eternal life?" (v. 25). How was this line of reasoning similar to the mistaken logic of the Jewish elders in 7:4-5?

3. Jesus could have said that eternal life comes from surrender and faith in him. Instead, Jesus raised a question on the lawyer's own terms. Why might this be an effective strategy for a proud man (v. 26)?

4. From boyhood, all rabbinic students were taught to recite Deuteronomy 6:5 both morning and evening. How could being asked to recite something he had learned as a boy have embarrassed this sophisticated lawyer whose intention was to trap Jesus?

5. Jesus told the lawyer that his answer was correct. Then he adds, "Do this and you will live." Why do you think the lawyer felt compelled to ask another question (v. 29)?

6. How do you think the lawyer would have answered his own clarifying question to Jesus (v. 29)?

This expert in Jewish law assumed he had obeyed the law and therefore qualified for eternal life. But Jesus showed him the impossibility of meeting the demands of the law by adding a scandalous twist to the parable of the good Samaritan. The hero in the story is a Samaritan, and Jewish people not only despised Samaritans but also refused to have any contact with them. The religious and racial animosity between Jews and Samaritans was profound and ugly. The action took place on a steep road that descended 3,300 feet from Jerusalem to Jericho—called "the red, bloody way." It was a very dangerous road because Jericho was a very wealthy city where two international trade routes crossed, and everyone who came had to pay customs. It was well known that violent gangs often attacked people on that road.

7. Describe the state of the victim in verse 30.

8. Why do you think the priest and the Levite didn't help this dying Jewish man (vv. 31-32)?

9. What did the Samaritan do when he arrived at the scene (vv. 33-35)?

10. How did the Samaritan demonstrate the meaning of "love your neighbor as yourself," even when the victim happened to be his most bitter enemy?

Given that the victim represented the poor and marginalized of his day, what further implications can you draw from this story about loving your neighbor as yourself?

11. How did the lawyer's answer to Jesus' question in verse 36 reveal his true feelings about the hero of the story (v. 37)?

12. Jesus told him to "go and do likewise." Do you think he would have been successful in loving his Samaritan neighbor as himself?

The lawyer believed that any Jew who obeyed the great Commandments (to love God and love one's neighbor with every fiber of one's being) would enter the kingdom of God. But the hitch is that no one can do it! Because sin has entered our planet, we are not able to live the loving, obedient lives that God requires. The Law points out our sin, but it cannot save us from sin. To live as God desires we need God's help.

Jesus with Mary and Martha: Read Luke 10:38-42.

Luke deliberately placed the story of Mary and Martha after the lawyer's story. Pay attention to how Jesus' response to Martha reveals the truth that the lawyer needed to hear. Jesus often visited this family of two sisters, Mary and Martha, and their brother, Lazarus—all of whom believed that Jesus was the promised Messiah. Jesus and his disciples were enjoying their hospitality in Bethany when a family conflict arose.

13. Notice what Mary is doing and what Martha is doing. Why do you think Martha interrupted Jesus' teaching with a complaint about her sister (v. 40)?

14. Jesus affectionately responded by saying, "Martha, Martha, . . . you are worried and upset about many things." Martha was sincerely trying to "love her neighbor," but she became anxious and fretful in the process. Jesus knows there are duties and responsibilities that must get done; he is talking about the importance of deciding wisely about life's paramount priorities. What was Jesus telling Martha that she had to put first when he said "only one thing is needed" (v. 42)?

15. Suppose the lawyer we read about earlier took up Jesus' challenge and set out to love God and his neighbor as never before. However, returning to Jesus discouraged, he said, "I tried to love my most bitter enemy, and I just couldn't do it. Where do I find the power to obey the law?" How does Jesus' response to Martha reveal the truth that the lawyer needed to hear?

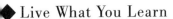

◆ Live What You Learn

16. Throughout the Gospels we see Jesus calling us to radically reassess our values, priorities and ambitions. Considering the story of Martha and Mary, how would your life be different if you replaced worry with worship?

FOUR

The God Who Finds the Lost

◆ **Discussion Starter**

Think of a time you lost something extremely valuable and precious. How did you feel? Was it returned? If so, describe your feelings.

◆ **Historical Context**

Jesus tells three powerful parables in this chapter: a seeking shepherd, a searching woman and a loving father. In this session we look at the first two parables. Remember that the interpretation of parables depends on whom Jesus was addressing. In this case the target audience was the Pharisees and teachers of the law who were complaining that Jesus was associating with riff-raff and sinners (15:2). Hearing their complaints, Jesus addressed their concerns through these three parables.

◆ Discovering Jesus

Jesus and the Parable of the Lost Sheep: Read Luke 15:1-7.

1. Describe the two groups Jesus was addressing (v. 1).

2. Why do you suppose Jesus attracted the despised tax collectors, prostitutes, lepers and other outcasts while other religious leaders did not?

3. What are all the things Jesus says a good shepherd does if one of his sheep is lost?

4. From verses 5 and 6 describe the response of the shepherd when he found what was lost.

5. Who do the lost sheep represent?

What does it mean to be "lost"?

6. How is the response of heaven (v. 7) similar to the response of the shepherd?

7. How would the response differ between the outcast tax collectors and the Pharisees upon hearing this parable?

Ezekiel 34:12 tells us that God is the shepherd who cares for us. God says, "As a shepherd looks after his scattered flock when he is with them, so I will look after my sheep. I will rescue them from all the places where they were scattered on a day of clouds and darkness."

The Parable of the Lost Coin: Read Luke 15:8-10.

8. What things did the woman do to find the missing coin?

9. What did she do when she found it?

10. What incredible thing was Jesus saying to the Pharisees about the nature and character of God?

11. What glimpse into heaven do these two parables give us?

12. Why did the religious group Jesus is addressing have difficulty seeing themselves as "lost" or in need of help?

◆ Live What You Learn

13. Jesus defends his association with sinners by saying that God truly loves people who are lost and confused. Why are "lost" people more likely to find God than the self-righteous?

FIVE

The God of Grace

◆ Discussion Starter

How would it change your life if you knew for certain that God is searching for you and loves you?

◆ Historical Context

There was a particular brand of Pharisees who were called "the bruised and bleeding" Pharisees. They were so committed to holiness that not only did they refuse to speak to a woman in public (to avoid the temptation of lust), but they refused to even look at a woman if she happened to walk by. This resulted in banging into walls in order to avoid temptation—thus the title "bruised and bleeding" described their appearance. Imagine their frustration with Jesus. He not only spoke with notorious sinners—he even ate meals with them! How, they wondered, could he possibly say that he came from God? Shouldn't a holy man be separated from the masses and take care to not be contaminated by sinful people?

Remember that the interpretation of parables depends on who Jesus was addressing. In this case the target audience is the Pharisees and teachers of the law who are complaining that Jesus is associating with riff-raff and sinners (15:2). Hearing their complaints, Jesus addresses their concerns through yet another parable—the result being one of the most beautiful portraits of God in the whole of Scripture.

As you read this parable, notice how Jesus deliberately pushes every orthodox Jewish button. It will be helpful to know that in the Jewish culture of Jesus' day an inheritance was normally given to sons after the death of the father. The younger son's share would be one-third and the older son's two-thirds of the father's wealth (Deuteronomy 21:17).

◆ Discovering Jesus

The Parable of the Lost Son: Read Luke 15:11-31.

1. How do you think the Jewish crowd listening to this scandalous story would feel about the younger son pushing for his share of the inheritance (vv. 11-12)?

2. What does the younger son reveal about his attitude toward his father and family with this request?

3. Jewish children in Jesus' day were raised to obey the law and to stay close as a family unit. The son moves to "a distant country" (v. 13) outside Jewish territory. How did the son's further antics reveal his disregard for his upbringing (vv. 13-16)?

4. In the parables of the lost sheep and coin, the owners searched until they found them. In this story the father let his son go. Why didn't he try to prevent his adult son from making disastrous choices?

Repentance in the Bible involves a change of mind (we agree with God and his ways) and a change of direction (our behavior matches our new beliefs). Repentance is often described biblically as "coming to one's senses."

5. Although what causes a person to repent and change is always a mystery, what factors seemed to influence the son finally coming to his senses in verse 17?

6. After hearing a story in which Jesus deliberately pressed all their buttons, what might the Pharisees and teachers of the law have expected the father's response to be?

7. What mixed feelings might the son have felt as he saw the family's estate in the distance?

8. Considering what we know of his situation, how do you think the son might have looked?

9. In verses 20-24 Jesus paints one of the most beautiful portraits of God the Father seen in the Bible. Name everything that the father in the story did.

10. How do you account for the fact that the father was watching just when the son arrived?

The banquet and the festivities meant that the father was reinstating his son in the community and his home. Jesus' point is that God is willing to bring an absolute reversal of status when we return and repent. The lost son had become a family member again. The father's acceptance of the remorseful son was total.

The Parable of the Elder Brother: Read Luke 15:25-31.

11. What were the reasons for the elder brother's anger toward his father (vv. 28-31)?

12. What did the elder son reveal as his motivation for serving his father (v. 29)?

13. The elder son refused to go to the party even after his father begged him. What was wrong with his understanding and experience of faith?

14. Remembering the divided audience who is listening to this parable, who do you think the elder brother represents?

The younger son?

15. What does this story teach us about the nature of God and his basis of acceptance, no matter what our past sins have been?

◆ Live What You Learn

16. It may have been difficult for the prodigal son to receive his father's lavish love when he knew he didn't deserve it. Why is God's grace (undeserved kindness and mercy) hard on our pride?

17. Jesus made it clear that while God searches for us and longs for us to come home to him, he will not violate our will. We must choose. In light of what we have learned about God's love for us, why do you think some of us choose to resist a God like this?

SIX

LUKE 18:35-19:11

The God Who Seeks the Seeker

◆ Discussion Starter

The Bible tells us: "You will seek me and find me when you seek me with all your heart" (Jeremiah 29:13). What do you think are the excuses or distractions we engage in that keep us from knowing God better?

◆ Historical Context

Jesus was on his way to Jerusalem to celebrate Passover, one of the most joyous times of the Jewish calendar year. Jesus, knowing the cross awaited him there, had just told his disciples for the seventh time that he was going to die as the Old Testament prophets had predicted (Luke 18:31-34). But his followers failed to understand. They assumed, like Nicodemus, that the Messiah would set up his earthly kingdom and free them from Rome, oust the Gentiles and inaugurate a new era. It must have been a lonely time for Jesus. Not only did his disciples not comprehend what awaited him, but also huge crowds accompanied him to Jerusalem who were full of joy and expectation that Jesus was about to set up "the kingdom of God" in Jerusalem (Luke 19:9).

Only a few days earlier Jesus had taught the parables of the lost sheep, lost coin and prodigal son to a group of tax collectors and sinners, telling them how the shepherd had left his ninety-nine safe sheep in order to search for one lost sheep (Luke 15:4-6). Now we are about to see Jesus being the Good Shepherd who seeks and saves the lost and maimed—whether they are rich or poor.

◆ Discovering Jesus

Jesus and the Blind Beggar: Read Luke 18:35-43.

1. As a blind man, his sense of hearing would have been especially well developed, thus he realized it was an unusually large crowd passing him by. What does his reaction tell us that he already believes about Jesus? (The phrase "Son of David" is another term for Messiah.)

2. Who do you suppose had told him about Jesus?

3. "Those who led the way" (v. 39) were no doubt the disciples. Why do you think they tried to silence the blind beggar?

4. Despite the crowd, Jesus' response to this man was totally different from that of his disciples (vv. 40-41). What did Jesus want his disciples to learn from his example?

5. Why did Jesus ask the man what he wanted him to do for him?

6. Jesus healed his blindness and said his faith was responsible for his healing. How was his faith demonstrated throughout the passage?

7. The beggar then set out to follow Jesus along the road to Jerusalem. What effect would his healing have had on his life and the lives of others?

The beggar gained his eyesight and a whole new productive life. He would never have to beg again. He joyfully followed Jesus to Jerusalem only to see him crucified on the cross. It is unimaginable to ponder the agony he experienced in being able to see the suffering of the One who had only just healed and restored him.

Jesus Encounters Zacchaeus the Tax Collector: Read Luke 19:1-9.

8. Find out all the facts you can about Zacchaeus from 19:1-4.

9. Try to picture what the crowd did when Jesus stopped and looked up into the tree. What feelings would Zacchaeus have had as he heard Jesus' words (19:3-6)?

10. The tax collectors were ostracized because they extorted money from fellow Jews for the Roman occupation forces. Why did Jesus risk his reputation by entering Zacchaeus's home (19:7)?

The religious leaders would object that Jesus had gone to eat in a home that was ceremonially unclean. To eat in that house would disqualify Jesus from eating the Passover meal without special cleansing rituals. The fact that Zacchaeus was so desperate to see Jesus, that he did not resist Jesus' offer to come to his home but received Jesus eagerly, suggests he was well on his way to becoming a true follower of Jesus. In verses 8-10 Jesus was in the home of Zacchaeus, no doubt eating a sumptuous meal that his host had provided.

11. What did Zacchaeus's formal announcement (19:8) reveal about his level of faith and repentance (see also Leviticus 6:1-5)?

12. What do you suppose Zacchaeus thought and felt as he heard Jesus say, "Today salvation has come to this house" (19:9)?

13. Verse 10 holds a surprise! Jesus was seeking Zacchaeus as well. Luke 5:27-30 shows us that Jesus had befriended tax collectors in the past. What two clues in 19:5 show that Jesus had also heard about Zacchaeus and had come looking for him?

14. God promises all seekers: "You will find me when you seek me with your whole heart" (Jeremiah 29:13). What qualities did the impoverished beggar have in common with the enormously wealthy but despised Zacchaeus, which allowed them to enter into the kingdom of God?

◆ Live What You Learn

Zacchaeus didn't know it, but that day in Jericho was his last chance! Jesus would die in a matter of days. What is clear from this story is that Jesus seeks us, softly calling us to get our attention.

15. What are ways in which you think God beckons or calls to us today?

The beautiful old hymn "I Sought the Lord" expresses the truth that God is the Hound of Heaven who seeks us and calls us to respond to him.

> I sought the Lord, and afterward I knew,
> He moved my soul to seek Him, seeking me.
> It was not I that found, O Savior true;
> No, I was found of Thee. (1880, Anonymous)

SEVEN

New Heart–New Hope

◆ **Discussion Starter**

What do you think is the source of our planet's misery, and what do you think is the cure?

◆ **Historical Context**

A very religious Jewish intellectual came to converse with Jesus one night. He was well educated and held a position of leadership in the Jewish community. He had a partial faith in Jesus and came seeking answers, no doubt expecting Jesus to give him more knowledge. But what Jesus offered as a solution wasn't information but *transformation*.

This is the most theological of all the passages we have read so far. It will take a little effort to understand what is being said, but it is well worth the effort!

◆ Discovering Jesus

Jesus and the Night Visitor: Read John 3:1-21.

1. Why do you think Nicodemus went to see Jesus at night?

2. What does verse 2 tell us about his attitude toward Jesus?

3. From his response in verse 3, what would you say Jesus seems to think Nicodemus is really concerned about?

Like other Jews of his time, Nicodemus was awaiting the kingdom of God that the Messiah would inaugurate. The Jews expected the Messiah to fulfill Old Testament prophecies and bring a new order in which God would reign and govern the world in fresh and miraculous ways. There would be a fresh outpouring of the Holy Spirit on men and women (Ezekiel 36:25-26; Joel 2:28-29).

But the Jews had misconstrued certain things. They expected the Messiah would liberate them politically from the hated Roman rule and domination. Furthermore, Nicodemus (a righteous Jew who observed the law) believed the only requirement for entering the kingdom of God was to be physically born a Jew and to be observant. What Jesus proclaimed to Nicodemus was that the long-awaited arrival of the kingdom of God had now come. However, the kingdom of God is spiritual in nature not political, and even righteous Jews must still be spiritually reborn.

4. To help Nicodemus understand his radical teaching, Jesus used contrasts. What meaning do you see in this contrasting of physical birth with spiritual birth (vv. 5-6)?

5. Jesus argued in verse 5 that, just as natural life begins when we are conceived by earthly parents, so eternal life begins when God the Father gives us his Holy Spirit. How did Jesus liken the Holy Spirit's activity in a person's spiritual life to the effect that wind has in the natural life (v. 8)?

6. From the exchange in verses 9-12, what is Nicodemus struggling to understand and accept about Jesus' spiritual teaching?

7. How did Jesus, who is often referred to as the Son of Man, defend his right to demand the faith and confidence of Nicodemus (vv. 13-16)?

To help Nicodemus understand, Jesus refers back to an Old Testament story in which a plague of poisonous snakes descended on the people because of their rebellion against God. God provided the cure by instructing Moses to craft a bronze snake and attach it to a pole. People who had been bitten didn't have to go to the temple, try to drain the poison or do any kind of religious "act." They were simply told to take God at his word, look at the snake and believe. Those who did were miraculously healed. Those who didn't died. (You can find this story in Numbers 21:4-9.) By using this metaphor for his own crucifixion, Jesus knew that Nicodemus would begin to grasp that God sent Jesus to earth so people could believe in him, receive forgiveness of their sins and have eternal life.

8. What parallels are there between Moses' pole and Christ's cross (vv. 14-15)?

9. What did Jesus say is God's motivation for providing such an extravagant remedy (the death of his Son) to save us from our sin (vv. 16-17)?

10. The gift of God's Spirit is primary to becoming spiritually reborn. What then are the conditions for receiving eternal life (vv. 16-18)?

How do these conditions contrast with the idea of gaining God's approval by doing good deeds only?

Nicodemus was a man for whom religion consisted of obeying a set of rules and trying hard to be good. But Jesus said that true faith is a relationship in which we worship the One whom God sent. It is only through faith and a radical surrender of our lives to Christ that we can receive the Holy Spirit and become the people God intended us to be. The wonderful news is that it appears Nicodemus became a follower of Jesus. It was Nicodemus who risked his life and reputation to anoint Christ's body after he died on the cross (John 19:38-41).

11. According to verses 19-21, why doesn't everyone believe in Jesus and receive eternal life?

12. How would you explain to someone unfamiliar with Christianity what it means to be "born again"?

◆ Live What You Learn

13. How would you describe where you are with Jesus at this point in your spiritual journey?

The apostle Paul explains the meaning of Jesus' cross in these words: "For in him [Christ] all the fulness of God was pleased to dwell, and through him to reconcile to himself all things, whether on earth or in heaven, making peace by the blood of his cross. And you, who once were estranged and hostile in mind, doing evil deeds, he has now reconciled in his body of flesh by his death, in order to present you holy and blameless and irreproachable before him" (Colossians 1:19-22 RSV).

"Therefore, if any one is in Christ, he is a new creation; the old has passed away, behold, the new has come. . . . For our sake he [God] made him to be sin who knew no sin, so that in him we might become the righteousness of God" (2 Corinthians 5:17, 21 RSV).

LEADER'S NOTES

Here's a little background on how the studies are put together and how to use each component.

Discussion Starter: Use this as an icebreaker to help people feel comfortable. The question addresses everyday concerns as well as an issue that relates to the biblical text. Why do we ask a general question first? Seekers often feel intimidated about reading the Bible. They are afraid their lack of Bible knowledge will show, or they feel hesitant to ask or give an honest response. But if *you* are relaxed and begin the study each week with a provocative question, it will lighten the atmosphere and make the participants feel at ease. Don't spend more than three minutes on the opening question. After discussing the question, there are several sentences you may read that will lead you into the "Historical Context" section.

Historical Context: This gives the participants some historical or cultural background in order to better understand the passage. Sometimes it merely explains what has happened in previous chapters. You may summarize the information or read it aloud while they read along with you (the participants should each have a guide). Remember, our role as leaders is not to be a "sage on the stage—but a guide on the side."

Discovering Jesus: These are questions that follow the inductive method. This is an approach that helps them discover, understand and correlate the facts in the text and discover for themselves what the Scripture is saying. One distinctive of a seeker Bible discussion is that the questions do not assume faith on the part of the participant. However, the questions engage the reader to look carefully at the text in order to understand its meaning.

Live What You Learn: These are the application questions. You will notice that as each week progresses the questions become a bit more focused and direct. Try to get through the passage so there's enough time to ask the application question. The more you get everyone participating in the conversation the better. Remember, however, to set the time for your study and stick to it. I would recommend no longer than sixty minutes.

Reading the Passage

You may wonder whether to read the entire passage first or read by sections and ask questions that pertain to each section. That depends on how long the passage is. In these studies I have broken each passage into sections so that you can read the Scripture in small units for better comprehension. Also, ask if anyone would like to read but don't call on someone to read. If no one offers to read then ask your coleader or read it yourself.

What to Do at Your First Study

There are two ways to start a study. One way is to have an introductory meeting. Keep it fun and offer light refreshments and introduce everyone to each other. Then explain your purpose in gathering, and select a time to gather that works for everyone. Then hand out the studies, and ask them to read the passage ahead of time if they wish. But assure them that "homework" isn't required. If they want to answer the questions in the guide they may; reading the text ahead of time will be helpful. But if they don't have time to do either, that's okay. You don't want them to stay away if they haven't read the passage, especially since you'll be reading it when you meet. Also discover if everyone has a Bible, and if they don't you can suggest a particular translation. I suggest RSV and NIV.

The other approach is to figure out through conversations which time seems to work for everyone and invite them to come. At the first meeting be sure you have extra Bibles. No one will have read the passage but that's okay. Before you study the passage, be sure to review the purpose for gathering and go over a few of the ground rules. Then after the study you may hand out the Bible study guide and tell them which passage you'll be reading for next time.

Whichever way you choose, here are things to cover in the first meeting:

1. Review the purpose for gathering (pp. 6-7).
2. Go over a few ground rules for discussion (p. 7).

3. Explain a few things about the Bible and Luke in particular (pp. 7-8).

4. Be sure everyone has a Bible.

STUDY 1. LUKE 7:1-17.
Finding Wholeness

Discussion Starter

On the positive side, sometimes our God-given blessings and gifts can keep us from seeing our need for God—beauty, wealth, great intellect can make us feel self-sufficient. On the other hand, negative things like suffering, the death of a loved one and illness can make us angry or bitter and cause us to doubt God.

Question 1

A centurion was a solider in Herod Antipas's army who commanded about one hundred men. He was a Gentile, but he was not a Roman since the Romans did not have military roles. Because he was in Capernaum, that means Capernaum was a Roman military station, there to maintain peace and order. To be so concerned for a slave reveals a kindhearted, compassionate-natured man.

Question 3

It is clear the centurion had enormous good will toward the Jews, given his support of the synagogue. However, it isn't clear whether he was a "proselyte" to Judaism. He was probably a "god-fearer," a Gentile who does not fully identify with Israel but does respect the God of Judaism. The Jewish commission tells Jesus that the centurion is "worthy" to receive the benefits of

Jesus' work because of his good deeds.

Clearly the centurion had heard about Jesus and his miracle-working power; perhaps he had even heard Jesus teach. His attitude toward Jesus was one of humility and profound respect. He made no demands, only a request. Even with his power and prestige, he recognized that he was unworthy to ask Jesus to come to his home. His humility is remarkable considering his own personal authority.

Question 4

In addition to his sensitivity to Jewish tradition, the centurion is showing that he knows that Jesus' authority was all that was needed to produce healing. Jesus didn't even have to be physically present! Clearly we see by Jesus' reaction to the centurion that his faith should be emulated.

Question 5

Jesus made it clear that it was the centurion's faith in him that made all the difference. Ephesians 2:8 says, "By grace you have been saved, through faith . . . not by works."

Question 7

Nain probably laid six miles southeast of Nazareth. There are only four resuscitation accounts in Luke-Acts (Lk 8:40-42; Acts 9:36-43; 20:7-12). The funeral process could not have begun until it was certain that the death had occurred. The contrast of the groups would have been painfully obvious between joy and extreme sorrow.

Question 8

This woman was without spouse or son, which meant she would have been destitute, with no family to care for her.

Question 9

Clearly Jesus was motivated by compassion. Since the Gospels never mention Joseph after the story of Mary and Joseph searching for Jesus as a boy in the temple, it is assumed that he died. No doubt Jesus was especially sensitive to a widow's sorrow having experienced it with his mother.

Question 13

Whether rich or poor, no human being has the power to give life to another. That is something only God can give.

Question 14

Note that the woman could have cried out to Jesus to not perform the miracle, that it was too late for her son was dead. She had a passive faith, and Jesus was willing to perform this spectacular miracle in the presence of even passive faith. It is when he encounters hostile unbelief that he cannot perform a miracle for it would be violating their will (as in the case of the country men who ask Jesus to leave after he healed the demoniac in Lk 8).

STUDY 2. LUKE 7:36–8:3.
Faith's Authentic Response

Question 2

The Pharisee had failed to do what was culturally accepted. People in those days walked everywhere in open sandals on dusty roads, so a servant always washed the feet of a guest. Also essential was a bit of scented olive oil dripped on the head, and if the guest was a friend or important, he would be given a kiss.

For Simon to have failed to do any of these things in a Middle Eastern culture that valued hospitality could not have been an oversight. Did Simon want to embarrass Jesus before his guests? Or was he worried about being judged by his pious friends for having invited such a controversial dinner guest?

Questions 3-4

Judging by the response of Simon, this woman was a well-known sinner. The shock was not that she came uninvited (it was common in the ancient world to have townspeople gather in the background when a major teaching figure was present) but that she drew so near to Jesus and that he allowed it. She is not to be confused with either Mary Magdalene who was from Magdala, or Mary of Bethany whose story is told in Mark 14:3 and Matthew 26:6. This unnamed woman lived in Capernaum.

She positioned herself at the foot end of Jesus' couch. There were probably enough people around at the tables that her presence was not noticed at first. The woman's actions reflect great cost, care and emotion. She didn't anoint Jesus' head but his *feet* with this costly perfume! Nevertheless, as her tears of joy and gratitude poured out, the undoing of her hair was culturally shocking. Any woman who went out in public with her long hair down and uncovered was considered a prostitute, and her kissing of Jesus' feet also expressed an intimacy shunned in this culture.

Question 5

She came because she had obviously heard that Jesus would be there. She brought her jar of alabaster because she wanted to anoint his head with her costly gift, as the perfume she used was expensive.

It's possible she wept because she had heard Jesus' message before and had been moved and transformed by it. However, it's also possible that she was grieved for how Simon had insulted Jesus.

Question 6

While her actions were offensive to the culture of her day it was her *heart* attitude that Jesus said was exemplary.

Question 9

It is important to notice that the tense in the verb in 7:47-48 is perfect. It is not "your sins are [at this moment] forgiven"; but "your sins have been [at some time in the past, however recently] forgiven." Evidently this woman had already heard Jesus teach, been saved by faith and had her sins forgiven.

Question 12

Her faith had saved her, not her love.

It is clear that she had received Jesus' message before she ever entered the room. But to be publicly pronounced forgiven means that every person in the room heard that Jesus saw her as a new woman. She could live a new life. The scope of salvation is not just spiritual but includes living a wholesome, godly, useful life. Now followers of Christ would include her as one of them.

STUDY 3. LUKE 10:25-42.
The Essence of True Religion

Question 1

Luke calls the man a lawyer; the Jews would have called him a scribe. Scribes interpreted Old Testament law and its application. The lawyer/scribe approached Jesus skeptically to "test him" to see if he was indeed the Messiah.

Question 2

His emphasis on "what must I *do*" is similar to the logic of the Jewish elders in 7:4-5 who believed the centurion merited Jesus' response because of his good works (whereas Jesus emphasized the man's faith).

Question 3

Jesus didn't answer the question . . . he raised one, a strategy he often employed. His questioner was a specialist in Jewish religious law, so Jesus asked a question on the man's own terms. The man had admitted that the law calls him to love God and his neighbor with the totality of his being. While it is theoretically true that "the man who practices the righteousness which is based on the law shall live by that righteousness" (Rom 10:5 NASB), the trouble is no one ever succeeds in doing so. That is why the Bible says " 'no human being will be justified in his sight' by deeds prescribed by the law" (Rom 3:20 NRSV).

Question 4

The first command is focused toward God (Deut 6:4-5), and it summarizes the first four of the Ten Commandments. The second is focused toward humanity (Lev 19:18), and it summarizes the last six commandments (Ex 20). Love for God is not a sentimental feeling but a heartfelt love that is demonstrated through willing obedience (Jn 14:21, 23). Loving others is to seek their highest good.

Question 5

The lawyer did not want to appear foolish and to have asked a simple question to which he already knew the answer. The lawyer's question "who is my neighbor?" was probably asked to appear theologically profound, but even if it was sincere, it poses an important issue. Who *is* my neighbor? Are we expected to treat every person we meet as our neighbor and love them as we love ourselves? Jesus' answer through the parable is yes—even if it's our bitter enemy.

Question 6

The lawyer would have assumed that he was to love fellow law-observing Jews and to remain separate from the "unclean," such as the Gentiles and Samaritans.

Question 8

The priest and the Levite had no compassion. They may not have worried about ritual purity because they were not going to Jerusalem to officiate, though the victim's probable loss of blood would have concerned them as it would have made them ceremonially unclean. No doubt they feared staying at a robbery and attempted murder scene. This shows the courage of the Samaritan all the more!

Question 10

In the immediate context our neighbor is anyone who touches our life and needs help. But the biblical call makes it clear that our "neighbor" also concerns those we may never meet personally—the poor, marginalized and disenfranchised. The biblical call is to care for and protect all human life.

Question 11

The lawyer couldn't even bring himself to say the word *Samaritan*; rather it was "the one who showed him mercy."

Question 13

Martha is "distracted" from listening to Jesus' teaching because she is no doubt trying to prepare an elaborate meal for her illustrious guest.

Question 14

At that moment listening to his teaching, being in his presence, was more important than doing things for him. There would be time to do the practical task of preparing the meal, at this moment she needed to quiet her heart and receive everything Jesus wanted to give her.

Question 15

Before we can be a "good Samaritan" to our neighbor, we must first meet the "Great Samaritan": Jesus Christ.

He is the one who will give us the resources and strength to love others as we must. The lawyer needed to hear that only through faith in Christ and receiving God's Spirit would he be strengthened to love God and his neighbor as himself.

Jesus says that to become the right sort of people who can begin to do the right sort of things we must put our faith in him first. Out of the gift of spiritual rebirth we are given the Holy Spirit who empowers us to live a life pleasing to God.

STUDY 4. LUKE 15:1-10.
The God Who Finds the Lost

Question 1

Jesus is speaking to a divided audience of separatist, self-righteous Pharisees and scribes (lawyers who interpret the law), and to outcasts and sinners. The tax collectors were appointed by the Romans and were generally hated for helping Rome. They frequently cheated the Jewish people by taking exorbitant amounts of money for themselves. "Sinners" included tax collectors, adulterers, robbers and those who did not follow the Mosaic law as it was interpreted by the teachers of the law. The Pharisees and scribes regarded the sinners as ceremonially unclean, which meant the sinners could contaminate them.

Question 2

Some sinners dared to come to Jesus because they had repented and been baptized by John. John had not ordered them to leave tax collecting but to no longer collect more than was fair. In Luke 5 Jesus chooses a tax collector, Levi, to be one of his inner circle, and he gave a lavish banquet to introduce his fellow tax collectors to Jesus. And of course, sinners came near to Jesus because they sensed his genuine compassion and love.

Question 5

The lost sheep represents a repentant seeker. The ninety-nine sheep represent all of the self-righteous, unrepentant, spiritually hostile religious people. Furthermore, these religious leaders would know that many of the messianic prophecies present Messiah as a shepherd or a shepherd-king. In John 10 Jesus claims to be the Good Shepherd who will look after his sheep. God came to care for his own. This parable shows accurately the loving relationship that Middle Eastern shepherds had with their sheep, knowing each one by name.

To be "lost" means to be lost to God, away from the Shepherd who loves you. It means to be on your own. To be "saved" means to be found by the Shepherd-King Jesus and brought home to the family where you can be loved and cared for.

Question 8

Why were these coins so important to this woman? The coin was a drachma, probably a day's wages. This would be a great loss to a poor woman. Some suggest it was part of a necklace she wore. In either case, the point was her great sense of loss.

Question 10

The first parable emphasizes the length to which the

shepherd will sacrifice to find the lost sheep. The second parable emphasizes the thoroughness of the search. The woman represents God searching for a lost treasure that he cares for a great deal. God cares about every lost person and makes a great effort to find them. No other religion has a God who makes such a great effort to find "lost" sinners.

Question 11

We learn that there are angels in heaven who throw a party whenever a lost one is found. These parables reveal heaven as a place of great joy!

STUDY 5. LUKE 15:11-31.
The God of Grace

Questions 1-2

The Jewish crowd would be outraged. When there were two sons, the elder received two portions and the younger only one, but they were to have no access to the inheritance until after the father's death. This was a grave insult. Receiving his portion at that time meant a third of all the family's wealth would be greatly reduced.

Question 3

The "distant country" (v. 13) was outside Jewish territory where they would not follow Jewish dietary laws. He had also been raised to obey God's moral laws, which he had clearly abandoned.

For any Jewish boy to be associated with pigs would be shocking and revolting to Jewish listeners, but especially to the ultra-conservative religious people Jesus was speaking to. Jesus was deliberately "pressing their religious buttons" with these kinds of details.

Questions 4-5

The parable shows that sin is often due to willful choice and a desire for indulgence. Jesus was unrelenting in showing us sin's deception, disillusionment, suffering, slavery and despair. One factor that may have led the boy to repent was the fact that the father didn't rescue him but allowed him to experience the consequences of his poor choices. Another factor may have been disgust and homesickness. He was no doubt appalled by how low he had sunk, and he had the memory of a former time of joy and plenty in his father's home.

Question 6

Many of the parables would have shocked their original audiences because they were often designed to overthrow existing values and prejudices. In this case, they expected the father of the story to be harsh and to expel the boy for such gross sin, whether he was repentant or not.

Question 9

The description of the son's return and the father's welcome is as vivid as that of his departure. Furthermore, the father saw him "while he was a long way off," perhaps because he was waiting or searching daily down the distant road hoping for his appearance. Some have pointed out that a father in that culture would not normally have run as he did. Everywhere there is evidence of compassion: the warm embrace, the kiss and so on.

The robe was a ceremonial one such as a guest of honor would be given, the ring signified authority, and the sandals were those only a free man would wear.

Question 13

The elder son's words characterize the self-righteousness of some of the Pharisees who criticized Jesus. The father's words indicate the possibilities that the elder son (or Pharisees) had never appreciated and the privileges he had never enjoyed. The elder son could have enjoyed the grace and love of God. Instead, religion had been an activity of rites and duties done from a sense of burden rather than a joyful heart. Instead of being grateful that God had pardoned his own sin and living in intimate relationship of devotion to his father, he obeyed his father's command out of a weary joylessness.

STUDY 6. LUKE 18:35–19:11.
The God Who Seeks the Seeker

Question 2

No doubt other blind people who had been healed by Jesus would have stopped and told him their stories.

Question 3

They would have assumed that this beggar was unimportant, a nobody, and certainly not worthy enough to interrupt someone as important as Jesus on his way to Jerusalem for Passover.

Question 4

We see that Jesus did not discriminate against the poor or the handicapped. In fact, he favored them. He came for them (Lk 4:18, 19). He wanted his disciples to develop similar compassion and to realize that everyone is someone to God.

Question 5

Jesus always wanted people to exercise their will and ask in faith for the thing they wanted. There needed to be specific requests for specific answers. Furthermore, this man was raised in a culture that believed that blindness and other disabilities were caused by some hidden sin that had made God reject him. He wanted healing, but he also wanted mercy and forgiveness.

Question 7

The disciples and the crowd would all thank and praise God along with the man. He would be another exhibit of Jesus' messianic power. In Mark 10:46-52 we are told that this blind beggar—Bartimaeus—was the son of Timaeus. This means that he became a well-known member of the early church.

Question 8

Rich Zacchaeus was a short Jewish man whose wealth had brought no sense of acceptance either with God or man. As a tax collector, he was despised by the Jews. Tax contractors and their employees collected for imperialist Rome. They were extortionists who overcharged and kept a very generous amount for themselves. He had to have discovered the hard way that money can't compensate for a lack of acceptance.

It is clear that Zacchaeus was desperate to have contact with Jesus. Almost certainly Zacchaeus had heard about Jesus through the tax-collector grapevine. They associated with each other, and many tax collectors had already repented and been baptized by John. Furthermore, Jesus had invited Matthew—a former tax collector—to be one of his disciples!

Question 11

The fact that Zacchaeus stood up to speak suggests that what he had to say was an important, formal announcement. Since Jewish law required restitution of only one and a fifth of the amount stolen (Lev 6:2-5), the fact that Zacchaeus wanted to repay four times that reveals his level of repentance. He was grieved that he had caused poverty to many. That he could give half his fortune to the poor, and also compensate those he cheated, shows how vastly wealthy he was.

Question 12

Zacchaeus may have already believed in Jesus based on the things he had heard about him. His restitution and repentance clearly evidenced his faith. What he lacked was a personal encounter with Jesus! He personally received Jesus into his home and his heart. To hear Jesus call him "a son of Abraham" meant he was a man of faith. Jesus did for him what all of his wealth could not do—Jesus gave him a sense of identity and acceptance.

Question 13

The fact that Jesus knew his name, knew that his home was big enough for his team and knew that he didn't already have guests suggests that he had inside information about Zacchaeus. It was important for Jesus to find lodging for himself and his team. A large number of houses in Jericho were owned by the wealthy high priests and Sanhedrin families. About a third of the Jewish priests lived there, already plotting to kill Jesus! They watched, but they would not follow Jesus into the house of such a scoundrel as Zacchaeus.

Jesus might have heard about Zacchaeus through the same tax-collector grapevine that helped Zacchaeus hear about Jesus! Probably Levi (see Lk 5:27-30) learned through an ex-colleague that Zacchaeus was a seeker, if not already a believer.

STUDY 7. JOHN 3:1-21.
New Heart—New Hope

Question 1

Nicodemus was a Pharisee, one who was devoted to obedience to the law of Moses in the Old Testament. Many of them thought God was pleased by rule-keeping more than by an attitude of love for God. Nicodemus was also a member of Israel's ruling religious council, the Sanhedrin. Nicodemus was a respected Bible scholar whom Jesus called "Israel's teacher." He might have come at night so that he wasn't seen by other Pharisees who disapproved of Jesus. It's also possible that it was easier to have a private talk at night.

Question 2

Nicodemus knew that Jesus was a teacher and that he had performed miracles. He also seemed to believe that Jesus had come from God as a prophet or messenger.

He came, no doubt, out of curiosity but also out of a spiritual hunger and emptiness. What exactly he believed when he left is not made clear.

Question 3

Jesus discerned the real, unspoken reason for this nocturnal visit: Nicodemus is searching for spiritual fulfillment ("kingdom of God").

Question 4

Jesus was telling him that his human accomplishments wouldn't give him eternal life or spiritual security. Life with God meant becoming a follower of Jesus by faith, not merely by being a good person. Nicodemus needed a life that centered on a relationship with God. Jesus called this new start being "born again."

Jesus used many metaphors to describe what would result when a person placed their trust in him. It was a powerful image that suggested the complete transformation that Jesus brought. Nicodemus would have put a great deal of trust in his first birth as a member of God's covenant people of Israel. But even the Old Testament revealed that more was needed than simply physical birth into Israel. Men and women needed a new heart—a transformed new life from God (Jer 31:33; Rom 3:28-29). But Nicodemus was struggling to understand how anything more could be required than physical birth as a Jew.

Jesus wanted Nicodemus to understand that the new birth is spiritual not physical. To be "born again" a person must be born physically from his parents (born of "water" and "flesh") and spiritually from God. Only God's Spirit can bring life to the human spirit. Entering God's kingdom requires God to give us his Spirit.

Question 5

We can see the effect of the wind, but we cannot see the wind itself. Likewise with the Spirit of God, we see (and so can others!) the effect God's Spirit is having in our lives by opening our spiritually blind eyes, softening our hearts, and strengthening our faith and character. But at its core it is a mystery.

Question 7

Jesus could speak authoritatively because he alone came down from heaven and was sent by God. He is God's one and only Son.

Question 8

All of us have suffered from the result of sin. Our problem is not that we are ignorant and in need of more education. We are spiritually broken and in need of a new life. Only by an act of faith could the Israelites be rescued from their sin. Likewise only through faith in Christ could Nicodemus's sins be pardoned and could he receive eternal life. Jesus was lifted up as the final sacrifice for human sin. When a person looks in faith to Christ, the person receives not what his or her sin deserves but what God, in grace, gives.

Question 9

We see that God is not an angry tyrant waiting to punish us at the slightest provocation. Jesus pictured God the Father as a God of mercy who sent his Son to die for human sin. God's primary attitude toward sinful human beings is not condemnation but love.

Question 10

Religious activity and good deeds are not what make us acceptable before God. We are made acceptable by faith alone. Good works flow from a heart of gratitude and love for all that God has done for us.

Question 11

God does not force salvation on anyone. He provided for us what we could not provide, but we must believe. Those who refuse God's grace demonstrate that they love the darkness more than the light.

Other Books by Rebecca Manley Pippert

Hope Has Its Reasons

This is a book geared for people who want honest answers to honest questions. Rebecca Pippert examines the persistently human longings that all of us share about significance, meaning, life and truth, and the search for security. Only after she unravels the core of the real problem that plagues us does she explore how Christ can meet our longings and solve our human crisis. There are no canned formulas or saccharine clichés. Realism rings in the stories she tells and the ideas she pursues. In doing so she leads us beyond the search for our own significance to the reasons for our hope in discovering God.

A Heart for God

How can God use the difficulties and sufferings in our lives to build character and deepen our faith? The biblical David faced some desperate circumstances and some tough choices. So do we, day by day. The author shows us how God is able to use the everyday grit and glory of our lives to shape a holy life within us. Using David as her guide she helps us understand the way Christian virtue is developed in our souls and vices are rooted out. We learn how we, like David, can choose the good, overcome temptation and grow to be one who has a heart for God.

Transformation

Would you like to move from despair to hope? Would you like to transform your feelings of fear to faith? Would you like to turn envy into compassion? The Bible shows how David turned these negative emotions in his life into godly character qualities. In this Christian Basics Bible Study, based on the Bible's account of David and the book *A Heart for God,* you'll investigate David's life, choices, mistakes and triumphs. Then you'll discover how you can make the same transformation in your own life.